The Campus History Series

UNIVERSITY OF TEXAS
AT AUSTIN
THE FIRST ONE HUNDRED YEARS

The Campus History Series

UNIVERSITY OF TEXAS AT AUSTIN
THE FIRST ONE HUNDRED YEARS

Lori Duran

ARCADIA
PUBLISHING

Published by Arcadia Publishing
Charleston, South Carolina

Printed in the United States of America

Library of Congress Control Number: 2020930228

For all general information, please contact Arcadia Publishing:
Telephone 843-853-2070
Fax 843-853-0044
E-mail sales@arcadiapublishing.com
For customer service and orders:
Toll-Free 1-888-313-2665

Visit us on the Internet at www.arcadiapublishing.com

For my daughters, Gabrielle and Lauren.
May they always enjoy learning.

CONTENTS

ACKNOWLEDGMENTS

I offer my sincere thanks and appreciation to my family and my husband, Juan, for the help and support I received while developing this book. Michael Miller and the staff of the Austin History Center provided guidance, advice, and assistance that made my research more productive than it ever could have been without them. The Austin History Center has been the primary historical research source for this book. Unless noted otherwise, the images appear courtesy of the Austin History Center. The image citations refer to the specific collection that contains the image. Some come from the General Collection and are identified as PICA, PICB, or PICH, or begin with AF. Other important collections used include the Neal Douglass Photography Collection (citations with ND), the Dewey Mears Collection (DM), and the Russell Chalberg Collection of Prints & Negatives (C).

I owe special thanks to the Texas Historical Commission for some of the photographs used in this book. I also want to especially thank Aryn Glazier and the staff of the Dolph Briscoe Center for American History for their photographs and assistance. Thank you to Mary Brady for her family photographs and helpfulness in this endeavor. Also thanks to Rob and Debbie Oliver, Brent Renfro, Lance Avery Morgan, Gary Susswein, Robin Grace Soto, and Forrest Preece for their contributions. I am most graciously appreciative of Allison Supancic at the Austin History Center, who encouraged me on while giving me great tips.

INTRODUCTION

Arriving in Austin in 1984 to attend graduate school at the University of Texas (UT), I had no idea I would later collect photographs and write about its history, but I was already interested in its background. Austin became my new home, and the university welcomed me with a scholarship and a meet-and-greet party for all the new students at the Institute of Latin American Studies. I went on to study a perhaps unusual combination of history, political science, and business administration. As I started my new life, I was fascinated by what had come before me and my time. Coming to Austin, I knew about the university's stellar academic reputation, especially in some fields. I also knew a little about the tower shooting incident, but not much. It has been rewarding to collect some resources that helped fill in my gaps of knowledge before 1984. Joe B. Frantz's *The Forty-Acre Follies* was particularly inspiring and insightful. Various other magazines and books helped me build a framework with which to understand UT's first 100 years. From this, I have organized my collection into five time periods: 1883–1919, 1919–1945, 1940–1960, 1960–1969, and 1970–1983.

The planning of the university started with the Republic of Texas, and the first manifestation of those plans shows up in 1883 with the opening of Old Main. For the first 40 years, the university remained mostly representative of the state's rural and small-town population. That Austin tenuously held on as the capital of Texas also helped the city win the University of Texas. The unpretentious start of this now grand university, still known as "the Forty Acres," was bounded by Guadalupe Street to the west and Speedway Street on the east along with Twenty-First and Twenty-Fourth Streets. It had just one building, constructed on top of College Hill, and even that was not completely ready in time for the first students. Over the next 34 years, the university added buildings, some substantial and others temporary structures. Overall, the look of the university was open spaces with few structures. But the earnest ambitions of the administration, faculty, and board of regents was to develop a first-rate university.

World War I and the discovery of oil on university-owned land prompted growth and a building boom. Even during the Great Depression, buildings were added to the university landscape, including a new Main Building, a student union (Texas Union), Hogg Memorial Auditorium, war memorials, gymnasiums, a stadium, and numerous classroom buildings and dormitories. A long-standing UT tradition, the Texas Relays, was started during these years and became Texas's contribution to track fever. Near the university, some noteworthy private businesses frequented by UT students, like Dirty Martin's KumBak Place and others on Guadalupe Street, also known as "the Drag," were already popular.

The aftermath of World War II and that tumultuous time further altered the look of the university. UT added a number of buildings and dormitories. A few popular traditions, such as Smokey the Cannon, the "hook 'em horns" hand sign, and the Big Bertha drum, originated during the postwar years. Having a Longhorn steer at football games started earlier but became cemented as a favorite tradition at this time. Guadalupe Street entertained students, fed them, and provided textbooks and other key supplies. The university also acquired some of its most memorable structures and statues during these years. A few professors introduced dramatic changes, and a couple of students made waves. One particularly noteworthy student started the university on the path to desegregation. Other alumni made headlines while advancing in their respective careers.

The 1960s brought exciting developments and one terrifying event that seems to be forever seared into national memory. The university added some notable buildings that are still recognizable today, including the largest dormitory in the United States. Statues added to the grounds added beauty to their settings. A legendary board of regents member and a former student who became the governor of Texas both lent their influence on the Forty Acres. Some great traditions were continued, and at least a couple were started during this decade marked by cultural change. By the end of the 1960s, there was at least one "love-in" that attracted university students, and the era produced Texas's first psychedelic club in Austin.

During the last 13 years of the school's first century (1970–1983), the university was starting to take on the look that it has today. Modern buildings replaced most of the older ones, and several famed icons of UT opened during this time. Students were involved in not only traditional activities but also new ones like antiwar protests. Esteemed scholars, orators, athletes, and their coaches contributed to university pride and garnered nationwide attention. Finally, a few campus area enterprises that are forever part of UT history left their mark on the campus area.

One

1883–1919

The University of Texas originated in 1839 when the Congress of the Republic of Texas set aside a 40-acre site, also known as "college hill," on the north side of Austin for a university. The Constitution of 1876 specified that the legislature, as soon as practicable, was to establish, organize, and provide for the maintenance and support of a "university of the first class" for the promotion of the study of literature and the arts and sciences. Starting with only one building, Old Main, for all functions, the university gradually grew to a handful of buildings in its first 40 years. Literature and the classics, chemistry, engineering, and law were taught from the beginning. Brackenridge Hall for men and the Woman's Building were the earliest residences and set the scene for many memorable occasions, as did the Peripatus, also known as "the Perip," a tree-lined walkway at the edge of campus. The earliest benefactors of the school gave resources that helped with building and housing. A couple of the oldest buildings that UT now uses were acquired by the university and became UT's Little Campus. Few early buildings remain today, but those that do, such as Battle and Sutton Halls, have astonishingly beautiful architectural details. Before the 1920s, many of the university's recognizable traditions and symbols were already established fan favorites. UT participated intensely in World War I, and out of this period, it developed the wartime School of Military Aeronautics. The students' protests over Gov. James E. "Pa" Ferguson were the earliest mass protests at the Forty Acres. Their opposition to some Ferguson policies and statements are noteworthy. But student life also had a sporty, and sometimes lighter, side with the beginnings of student activities such as the Curtain Club, the early baseball and football programs, and the Varsity Circus. The school song, school colors, and mascot were already being sorted out. The rivalry between UT and Texas A&M was already strong. The football feud, as well as the teasing back and forth between the students of those two universities, was heating up before the end of the 19th century.

This singular edifice was the entire University of Texas when it opened, and it would be the west wing of Main Building when construction was completed years later. The University of Texas opened in September 1883, but due to financial constraints, there was a construction delay, and the building was not ready in time for the students. So classes were held in the temporary capitol building that semester. The Senate Chamber was used for assembly hall, and the Hall of Representatives was partitioned for use as lecture rooms. The construction finally finished later that year, and the university moved into Main Building in 1884. This building was expanded in the following years, and over time, became known as Old Main. (C06713.)

UT's original Main Building was completed in 1899. The structure was built in three stages. The west wing was completed during the 1883–1884 school year for the university's first class of 221 students. The central section was completed in 1891, and finally, the east wing was finished in 1899. Old Main featured wide corridors, high rotundas, a 2,000-seat grand auditorium, a library, a chapel, 9 lecture halls, 30 classrooms, and even a dressing room for women. Here, students and faculty walk on the sidewalks and lounge on the grass in front of the building. In 1932, a mere 33 years after the building was completed, the university announced the planned demolition of Old Main in favor of a new administration-library building. Protests from faculty, students, and residents of Austin arose, but with the integrity of the auditorium roof compromised due to a design flaw, the building's life expectancy was limited. (PICA 08451.)

The oldest building still standing at the university was built in 1857 as the Blind Asylum. In 1865, at the end of the Civil War, Union general George Armstrong Custer and his wife, Elizabeth, moved in temporarily at the invitation of the governor. Eventually, the Custers moved on, and the building served multiple purposes over the years. In the 1883–1884 City of Austin Directory, the building is listed as the Texas Institute of Learning for the Blind. The asylum structure eventually became part of Little Campus, a handful of buildings on the south side of the university. The Little Campus complex was transferred permanently to the university by the end of 1926 and was used for a wide variety of purposes. (PICA 18261.)

This 1891 building, also located on the Little Campus, was renamed in honor of John W. Hargis, the first African American to receive an undergraduate degree in chemical engineering at UT. Hargis Hall is a two-story Victorian Italianate structure formed by joining two buildings; it is one of the oldest buildings on campus. The building was acquired by the university in 1926 and served as a men's dormitory, and later as the human resources office. Hargis attended Morehouse College in Atlanta where he studied medicine. After deciding to become an engineer instead, he attempted to enroll at the University of Texas in 1954 but was told to take additional courses at Prairie View A&M University. In 1955, he was finally admitted to the University of Texas and graduated in 1959. (Author's collection.)

George Washington Littlefield was a benefactor to UT and gave the Wren Library and financing for structures such as the Littlefield Memorial Fountain (a World War I monument) and Littlefield Hall, a dormitory for women. His largesse included statues of Southern men, mostly linked to the Confederacy, that were originally placed along Main Mall; years later, all but one of them were moved into storage. Littlefield was a university regent from 1911 to 1920. (PICB 12233.)

Perhaps Littlefield's most personal gift to the university was his 17-room residence, built in 1893 at Twenty-Fourth Street and Whitis Avenue. Littlefield died at this house in November 1920. Following the death of his wife, the house was left to the university in 1935. It was intended to be the university president's house but instead was used for other purposes over the years, such as for the ex-students association, Naval Reserve Officers' Training Corps (ROTC), and a music practice hall. (The Texas Historical Commission.)

The Littlefield Carriage House has been used extensively by the communications department. From 1939 and into the 1950s, this was known as the Radio House, where students trained in speaking, acting, script writing, and using technology for careers in radio and television. (Author's collection.)

Three female students are sitting among the bluebonnets. At one time, open spaces around Old Main were covered in bluebonnets each spring. In the background are the Woman's Building on the left, constructed in 1903, and the old Chemical Laboratory, built 1892. Both were destroyed by fire; the Woman's Building burned in 1959, and the Chemical Laboratory in 1926. (C00691.)

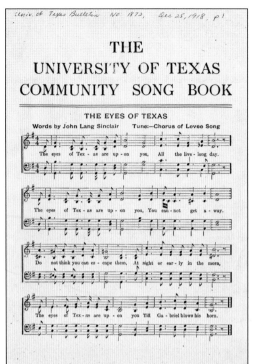

Univ. of Texas Bulletin No. 1872, Dec 25, 1918, p1

THE UNIVERSITY OF TEXAS COMMUNITY SONG BOOK

THE EYES OF TEXAS

Words by John Lang Sinclair   Tune:—Chorus of Levee Song

The eyes of Tex - as are up - on you, All the live - long day.

The eyes of Tex - as are up - on you, You can - not get a - way.

Do not think you can es - cape them, At night or ear - ly in the morn,

The eyes of Tex - as are up - on you Till Ga - briel blows his horn.

This is the sheet music for the UT school song, "The Eyes of Texas." It dates to 1899, when university president William Prather said, "Students of the University of Texas, the eyes of Texas are upon you." In 1903, student John Lang Sinclair created lyrics from the quote and set it to the tune of "I've Been Working on the Railroad." The song became the rallying cry of the university. (AF-M9370-001.)

On March 2, 1897, this cannon was fired by Tom Connally of Brackenridge Hall (B-Hall) to celebrate Texas's independence from Mexico. Opened in 1890 as men's dormitory, B-Hall was constructed with funds donated by George Brackenridge. It operated for almost 30 years before being repurposed and later demolished. B-Hall residents were known for mischievous hijinks, such as kidnapping the South Austin Fulmore School bell and requiring freshmen to make a nighttime dash from the dormitory to the capitol and back in underwear. (PICA 19418.)

The Woman's Building, shown here in 1903, was the first UT residence hall for women. The capacity was 86, along with head matron Asenath Carothers, in mostly single rooms. Students enjoyed their own dining room and parlor and a full gymnasium in the basement, which included a pool, elevated running track, and basketball court. Some of the first basketball games at UT were played by women in this building. They had a strict 10:00 p.m. curfew and needed a chaperone for their dates. With all of its features and amenities, the Woman's Building remained a desirable dormitory for the next 55 years. (Mary Brady.)

Dated 1910–1917, this photograph shows a young woman sitting at the top of the impressive staircase of the Woman's Building. The windows and stonework on either side of the entrance sport some ivy. The building burned down in 1959. Today, Flawn Academic Center stands at the same location. (PICA 07945.)

The Chemical Laboratory was built in 1892. This was the third permanent building on campus, sitting about where the Biological Sciences greenhouses now stand. Prior to this building, laboratories were allotted space in the basement of Old Main; however, concerns over fire risks prompted the construction of a separate laboratory building almost immediately. A regents' report from December 1884 mentioned that the noxious and disagreeable gases involved in chemical work permeated nearby rooms. Unfortunately, this building caught fire and burned down in 1926. (C00175.)

The Peripatus, or "the Perip," is shown looking north at Twenty-First Street in 1904. This tree-lined walkway at the edge of campus was a popular place for couples to stroll and friends to meet in the days before students had cars. George Littlefield, students, professors, and businesses contributed funds to build the Peripatus in 1901. University physics professor John Kuehne took this photograph. (Barker History Center and the Austin History Center, PICA 07931.)

ENGINEERING BUILDING, UNIVERSITY OF TEXAS, AUSTIN, TEXAS.

The original Engineering Building was built in 1904. The College of Engineering was officially established in the 1890s. When a new structure was built later, this building was converted into the Speech Building. During the installation of an elevator in 1991, it was found to be unsafe, and a recommendation was made to condemn it. Narrowly escaping the wrecking ball, it underwent extensive renovations beginning in 1997. In recent years, it has housed the administrative offices of the College of Liberal Arts. The building is now named after Dorothy L. Gebauer, former dean of women and a driving force in campus life for several decades. (AF-P6150 [45] [017].)

This statue of Texas governor James Stephen Hogg (1851–1906) is now located in front of the Will C. Hogg Building, named for his son. Governor Hogg was the first native-born Texas governor. Various members of the prosperous and civic-minded Hogg family were students and benefactors of UT. The Hogg statue was removed from the university's South Mall in 2017 along with three statues of Confederate figures that had been gifts of George Littlefield. Will C. Hogg earned his law degree from UT Austin in 1897, served as a regent, and helped found the alumni association. (Author's collection.)

The campus is seen in this 1906 postcard. The university still relied on Old Main (right) for many of its classes, administration, and other functions. The campus water tank can be seen in the background at center. (AF-P6150 [45] [011].)

The rapid growth of the university required the building of temporary classroom structures, nicknamed "shacks," as seen here just before World War I. Built inexpensively, the shacks were known as being furnaces in the warm months, and heavy rains could make them very unpleasant. In the 1920s, UT's oil revenue made it possible to tear down the shacks and build more substantial buildings. (PICA 07914.)

Pearce Hall, the old law building, was constructed at the intersection of Twenty-First and Speedway Streets. Construction began in December 1906 and was finished in November 1908. Before that time, law school classes were held in the basement of Old Main. Years later, Pearce Hall was replaced by Townes Hall, which was dedicated in 1953, and the new law library was named in honor of Judge Benjamin Tarlton. (PICA 07899.)

Titled "As We Turn Them Out," this illustration of a sophisticate in the 1896 *Cactus* yearbook seems ironic since most of the students then were from farms and small towns. This image also invokes the nickname "tea-sippers," which was applied to UT students by those of Texas A&M University, also known as the Aggies. Supposedly, well-to-do students of UT turned out to be doctors, lawyers, and the like, while A&M was the assumed blue-collar school, which traditionally taught agriculture and mechanics. (The Flower Hill Foundation.)

The 1899 law graduates are shown in this class photograph. The University of Texas at Austin's Department of Law began when the university was founded in 1883, with two professors and 52 students in the basement of Old Main. Lawrence Kelley Smoot graduated from the law school at age 20 and is pictured at far left in the second row from the top. (The Flower Hill Foundation.)

Until the university had its own auditorium, Millett Opera House on Ninth Street was used for various functions. This is where the first graduates, including 13 law school graduates, walked the stage to accept their diplomas. Both the 1878 opera house and the nearby Driskill Hotel were used for social events, balls, and other school exercises, and both still stand today. (C00123.)

This building was created for the School of Education and university administration in 1918. In 1930, it was named after William Seneca Sutton, the first dean. Sutton Hall today is used by the School of Architecture. (PICA 07763.)

This 1980 photograph showcases the rich details on Sutton Hall. The building's design was also practical, as thin rectangular buildings proved well suited to cross-ventilating breezes and natural illumination. Other nearby buildings, like Battle Hall, also feature elaborate designs and intricate details. (The Texas Historical Commission.)

William Seneca Sutton is shown here in 1896, just before he moved from Houston to Austin where he first became an instructor in education at the University of Texas. Sutton was also an author, and in 1909, he became dean of the School of Education before becoming acting president of UT in 1923–1924. (PICB 08767.)

Battle Hall, seen in this undated photograph, was built in 1911 to be the university library, and later became the first home of the Barker Texas History Center. In 1973, it was renamed after W.J. Battle, a professor of classics from 1893 to 1948. Battle also served as UT president ad interim from 1914 to 1916. (C06858.)

This photograph was taken looking south toward the Texas capitol from Main Building, which was built on a rise in the land ("College Hill") north of the capitol. An unpaved University Avenue is in view. The university was built on 40 acres north of Austin that had been set aside since the days of the republic. (C00140.)

This 1916 postcard of the campus captures the sparsity of buildings, the dirt pathways, and the large green open spaces of the early era. The university provided instruction in chemistry, physics, mathematics, ancient languages, English, history, literature, mental and moral philosophy, political science, modern languages, and law. (AF-P6150 [45] [010].)

This view of the university from a distance illustrates how the neighborhood around the campus was also sparsely settled. The original campus was mostly prairie, with thickets of weeds, trees, and cow trails. In 1905, the City of Austin had 25,299 inhabitants. The university had 1,357 students, and it struggled with finances and resources. (AF-P6150 [45] [012].)

Three young men, dressed in military uniforms, are sitting on the lawn in front of Old Main. From left to right are Curry, Hart, and Callender. The entire campus was involved and influenced by the war effort during World War I. Geraldine Hill, who attended UT during this time, reported that it seemed like a women's college because so many of the men were noticeably absent. The phrase "Berlin or Bust" was a popular wartime slogan. (PICA 08064.)

During World War I, UT operated a school for military aeronautics, a school for radio operators, and one for automobile mechanics. Also, an ROTC was established. Numerous students left their academic pursuits for the military. From the College of Arts alone, 400 students withdrew. The Little Campus was used for World War II as well, and during both wars, the sight of soldiers marching through campus was very common. (PICA 08045.)

Squad No. 36 of the School of Military Aeronautics is standing on the steps in front of the state capitol. The university's involvement in World War I affected all departments. In the spring of 1917, a total of 500 men left the university for officers' training camp. It was said that the law school was nearly depleted. In the immediate aftermath of the war , there was a huge wave of male students, and the university responded with year-round classes and a second commencement. (PICA 08057.)

Preparing to protest against Governor Ferguson, university students and supporters gather on the lawn behind Old Main in 1917. Ferguson controversially vetoed appropriations for the University of Texas and made charges against the university and its leadership after clashing with the regents. The students were protesting those issues as well as Ferguson's directive to ban fraternities and sororities from UT. He was impeached and removed from office by the Texas legislature later that year. (PICA 08003.)

These 1905 Curtain Club members are, from left to right, Maurice Wolf, George Norrell, Charles Casey, and Alf Toombs. The theatrical society and performing group has been a popular student organization for many years. Zachary Scott, John and Nellie Connelly, Rip Torn, and Tommy Tune were once members. In 1959, the club celebrated its 50th anniversary by staging *Teahouse of the August Moon*. The old Modern Language Building was next door to Hogg Auditorium, and it housed the shop where scenery was constructed. Unfortunately, it burned down in 1959, heralding the beginning of the end for the Curtain Club. The organization gradually lost its importance and identity in the 1960s. (PICA 13251.)

To help finance the university baseball program, students hosted a fundraiser in the form of a circus performance, dubbed the Varsity Circus. The entire campus pitched in with organization and preparations. The Varsity Circus included elephant costumes, as seen here. For 10¢, spectators could get a glimpse of the bearded lady, the human frog, the wild man, and other curiosities. (PICA 08082.)

The Varsity Circus raised enough funds to retire the athletics debt and provide generous contributions to the band and the glee club. With this success, the University of Texas baseball team continued, and the Varsity Circus became a tradition into the 1920s. (PICA 08086.)

In 1927, the new Clark Field was rebuilt where Bass Concert Hall is today, replacing the earlier site near Twenty-Fourth and Speedway Streets. The new Clark Field was used primarily for baseball, as football and track were moved to Memorial Stadium. Some alumni recall that opposing teams were undermined and had to scramble due to the rock ledge and rise in the backfield of the new Clark Field. The field was still in use until the early 1970s. (C07758.)

Billy Disch, shown in 1928, was a successful baseball coach, beginning his nearly 30-year career in 1911. Disch won 465 collegiate games during his Longhorn years. Bibb Falk followed him, and the Longhorns won 434 games during his tenure from about 1942 to 1967. Both coaches had such a reputation that they did not need to recruit. Instead, ambitious baseball players came to them. In 1972, the board of regents moved the baseball field to UT property in east Austin, which was named Disch-Falk Field and opened officially in 1975. (C07560.)

This undated photograph shows a football game at Clark Field. Football was still in its infancy when UT began its program in 1893. In the early 1900s, a sportswriter called the team "the Longhorns." In 1913, the team received warm-up blankets with "Longhorns" sewn on them. That act seemed to cement the longhorn as a symbol of UT. Three years later, a longhorn steer was brought out onto the field during a game and became the mascot thereafter. Years later, the name Bevo was applied to UT's mascot. There are various theories of how the name came about. Most likely, it had to do with the name of a popular near-beer that was imbibed by students during the era of impending Prohibition. (PICA 08141.)

These three UT football players are wearing stripes, quilted pants, and laced ankle boots. In 1899, the football schedule included schools such as Texas A&M, Sewanee, Vanderbilt, Tulane, and Louisiana State. In the late 1800s, fans were requested to wear ribbons to represent the school at out-of-town games. Only orange and white ribbons were available at a local store. Orange seemed to grow on the Longhorn fans, but for some years, the university's athletic teams tried different shades of orange and even different colors. Finally, the regents took a vote of alumni, faculty, and students, which turned out in favor of orange and white. For years, a brighter shade of orange was used until mid-century, when football coach Darrell Royal insisted that burnt orange held up better on football jerseys after repeated launderings. (PICA 08157.)

Paul Simmonds is shown being tackled in a 30-7 loss to Notre Dame on Thanksgiving Day 1913. UT has played Texas A&M intermittently on Thanksgiving, and that quickly became a favorite and heavily attended game for both teams. The Thanksgiving game became part of the legacy for both schools. (C05106.)

Two

1919–1945

The years between 1919 and the end of World War II saw tremendous change at the University of Texas. Old Main was replaced with a grand building that featured one of the few tower structures then in Austin. That tower quickly became the most recognizable symbol of the university. Oil was discovered on university-owned West Texas land. Other iconic UT buildings and structures were built on campus, such as the Texas Union, Goldsmith Hall, Garrison Hall, the Biological Laboratories building, Waggener Hall, Mary Gearing Hall, Hogg Auditorium, Welch Hall, Memorial Stadium, Littlefield Memorial Fountain, Anna Hiss and Gregory gymnasiums, a well-loved pond, and dormitories. One university president made headlines when he was at odds with the board of regents, and the controversy spilled over into student protests. Nearby private businesses along the Drag and farther north on Guadalupe Street catered to the college population. The YMCA on Guadalupe provided student meeting spaces, Bible study, and fellowship. The famed Texas Relays was the promotional creation of Clyde Littlefield. Memorial Stadium was built and became the home of the Longhorn football and track teams. During the same years, the student population grew tremendously. The increasing numbers of female students was remarkable. Women had always made up a portion of the student body. The university became one of Austin's most prominent cultural institutions, with families like the Smoots of Austin sending multiple generations to UT.

LITTLEFIELD MEMORIAL FOUNTAIN, MAIN BUILDING AND LIBRARY, UNIVERSITY OF TEXAS, AUSTIN, TEXAS

The 1932 Littlefield Memorial Fountain with the current Main Building in the background made for an attractive entrance to the university. Due to design issues, especially in the auditoriums, Old Main was replaced with a new building. The auditorium had been closed for some time as it was deemed unsafe. Since many classrooms were also inside Old Main, students and faculty were at risk. Additionally, at the close of World War I, the student population surged. It was determined that a new building would best serve the needs of the university. (AF-P6150 [45] [008].)

"The Tower" University of Texas
Photo by Ellison, Austin

This view is looking north at the new Main Building from Nineteenth Street. Old Main was demolished and replaced with this new structure during 1934–1935. The new Main Building was financed with a Public Works Administration grant and housed administration and a library. The reading room's ceiling timbers had lofty quotes painted on them. It was intended to be the state's biggest library. The students requested books from librarians, who pulled them from an upper floor and sent them down on a dumbwaiter. This building, with its striking tall tower, has become the most recognizable symbol of the university. Orange and white lights illuminate it for school victories and special occasions. In 1947, Carl J. Eckhardt Jr. helped create guidelines for using the orange lights. A number "1" on all sides highlighted by orange lights signaled that the university won a national championship. The full tower glowing orange represented a victory over Texas A&M, commencement, or other occasions the president deemed appropriate. The tower top bathed in orange symbolized other victories or a conference title in any intercollegiate sport. (C03474.)

Main Entrance to University of Texas, Austin, Texas

OB-H53

Despite the renovations on campus since this photograph was taken, this entrance is still recognizable today. The flower bed spelling out "UT" is gone and replaced by sidewalks, retaining walls, and steps. Today, there is a large stone sign. But the Texas Union, Administration, and Architectural Buildings are still there and look the same from this perspective on Guadalupe Street. (AF-P6150 [45] [014].)

UT Longhorn track coach Clyde Littlefield inaugurated the Texas Relays on March 27, 1925, drawing to Austin some of the best college track athletes. This major annual national track-and-field event was held at Memorial Stadium. In 1927, six Tarahumara runners from northern Mexico participated, partly as a savvy promotion for the event. Known for their exceptional long-distance running, they competed in various events. Two of the men completed a run from San Antonio City Hall to Memorial Stadium, nearly 90 miles. Littlefield was a former UT basketball and football player and track star. His career at UT included coaching track from 1920 to 1961, winning 25 Southwest Conference championships. The Texas Relays started as a small, regional competition, but has grown into one of the nation's most important meets. (PICA 19556.)

Geraldine Hill is pictured in front of the Tau Deuteron "Figi" House as a student at UT in 1919. This house was used for women's housing during World War I. The grand residence, built in 1902, became the home of Tau Deuteron through the family of H.J. Lutcher Stark, who bought the Goldbeck mansion. (Mary Brady.)

Geraldine Hill (center) and friends are pictured on campus in 1919. In 1883, women made up approximately 26 percent of the student body. Hill was born in East Texas, attended UT, and went on to teach high school in Fort Worth. She also took graduate courses at Columbia University. She is remembered for being generous, leaving the majority of her estate to UT, creating scholarships for deserving students in the College of Liberal Arts. (Mary Brady.)

Lawrence Kelley Smoot graduated from UT law school in 1899 and went on to work as the state law librarian. Later, he was an editorial reporter for the Texas Supreme Court for 66 years. (The Flower Hill Foundation.)

Another Smoot family member, Dr. Amelia Worthington Williams, got her doctorate in history from UT in 1935 and then joined the faculty as a history professor. During her UT tenure, she was considered the foremost authority on the Alamo. (The Flower Hill Foundation.)

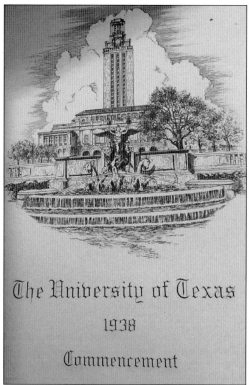

The University of Texas

1938

Commencement

This was the commencement program given to Jane Smoot in 1938. The daughter of Lawrence Kelley Smoot, she was born in 1919 and graduated from UT in 1938. She earned her master's the following year and then began a long career teaching at Austin Independent School District, including at the university's junior high. In addition, she spent two and a half years teaching veterans at UT who had returned home after World War II. The university needed the help, as by 1947, nearly half of college admissions were veterans. (The Flower Hill Foundation.)

This greenhouse and small oasis of nature is situated where most of the surrounding buildings were built in the 1920s and 1930s, just north of Main Building and its tower and adjacent to the Turtle Pond, the Biological Laboratories building, and Hogg Auditorium. (Author's collection.)

The new Brackenridge Hall was built in 1933 and replaced the original legendary B-Hall, also named after George Brackenridge. The new residence, shown here in 1980, is farther from the main Administration Building than the original Brackenridge, as it resides in the Waller Creek Community close to UT RecSports and dormitory dining facilities. (The Texas Historical Commission.)

Garrison Hall was built in 1926. Shown here in 1980, it is named after George Garrison, who joined the university in 1884 and was the first chair of the history department and a founding member of the Texas State Historical Association. Limestone carvings of Western symbols, such as Longhorn skulls and cactus, decorate the entrances. Imprinted below the eaves and corner windows are the names of founders of the Republic of Texas. Cattle brands adorn the outer stone walls. (The Texas Historical Commission.)

The Biological Laboratories building was built in 1924. In 1899, both biology, zoology, and botany moved onto the third floor of Old Main, sharing it with the School of Geology until 1925. With constitutional amendments and oil money, UT decided to construct a new building to house zoology and botany in the 1920s. In 1925, both left the bat-infested Old Main for their new home in the Biological Laboratories building, which still stands. (Author's collection.)

Paul Cret designed the Texas Union, built in 1933. Cret also designed the tower and Main Building, Goldsmith Hall, Texas Memorial Museum, and others on campus. Texas Union was constructed with funds provided by a Texas Exes campaign. Above an entrance still labeled "The Commons" are symbols that represent the university. The Texas Union was extensively renovated in 1976. (The Texas Historical Commission.)

This is the entrance to a ballroom inside the historic Texas Union building. The union was built to be a living room for students at a time when most of them lived on campus or very close. This ballroom has been the site of many functions over the years.(Author's collection.)

Waggener Hall is named after former president Leslie Waggener, who served as first chairman of the faculty from 1884 to 1894 and president ad interim the following year. The building was once occupied by the School of Business, and later the Department of Philosophy and the Department of Classics and the Classics Library. (Author's collection.)

Carothers Dormitory, built in 1937, is named in honor of Asenath Carothers, who became the director of the Woman's Building in 1903. This dorm was built in a Spanish Renaissance style. UT alumnus Debbie Oliver remembers that, when she lived in this dormitory in the late 1970s, it still did not have air-conditioning. Oliver also recalls that dormitory dances were fun in the 1970s, and residents set up for them by pushing the tables and chairs out of the way in the common areas. (Author's collection.)

Littlefield Hall for women was built in 1927 using funds donated by UT benefactor George Littlefield. It is UT's oldest residence hall, and is full of history and tradition. Residents have a patio café, and have their own mascot, colors, and song. (The Texas Historical Commission.)

Mary Gearing Hall, also known as the Home Economics Building, was built in 1932. One of this department's most famous instructors, Helen Corbitt, arrived in 1940 to teach large-scale cooking and tearoom management. She managed a university teahouse inside a small cottage along nearby Waller Creek. The teahouse is long gone, but Mary Gearing Hall still stands. Corbitt went on to a long culinary career at the Driskill Hotel, the Houston Country Club, and Neiman Marcus. (The Texas Historical Commission.)

Hogg Auditorium, shown here in 1980, was built in 1932. It was home to the Curtain Club and was the main stage for UT's drama department. It has also served as a venue for lectures, debates, and traveling plays. It was the first theater on campus and was one of the structures financed largely by student and alumni efforts. The auditorium was named after James Stephen Hogg, the first native governor of Texas. (The Texas Historical Commission.)

University of Texas, Y. M. C. A. Building, Austin, Texas.

The University of Texas YMCA was once at the corner of Twenty-Second and Guadalupe Streets. This large building was erected in 1912 following donation drives. During the 1960s and 1970s, student activists met there before it was closed in the late 1970s. Former students recall that, within the last few years of the 1970s, the Chuckwagon was closed, the student union underwent a long process of remodeling, and the former Methodist Student Center was also gone. Thus, most of the regular places for student-led political discussions were eradicated. (AF-P6150 [45] [016].)

In 1978, UT's Architecture Building was renamed for former professor of architecture Goldwin Goldsmith. Built in 1932, Goldsmith Hall was designed by Paul Cret, who would go on to collaborate on about 20 buildings on campus. (C06728.)

The Chemistry Building was constructed on Twenty-Fourth Street in 1930 after the earlier building burned down. Two additional wings were added in 1959 and 1974, and it was renamed Welch Hall in 1974. Chemistry was one of the earliest disciplines at the university. (C07540.)

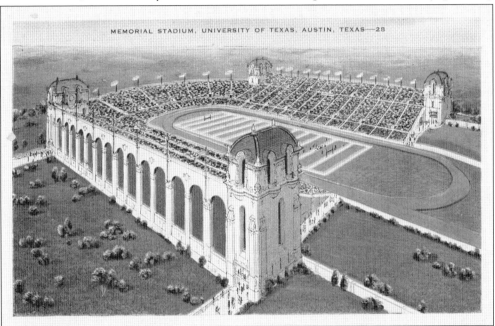

This postcard depicts the plans for Memorial Stadium, including the turrets that were not constructed. The back reads, "The first concrete stadium in the southwest is being built by students, ex-students and friends of UT as a memorial to those who served in World War I. Construction began in 1924. The completed stadium is used for football and will seat 50,000 fans." An estimated 10,000 students, alumni, and friends of the university gave money to build the facility. It was designed as a dual-purpose facility with a running track surrounding the football field. The skeleton of this original structure still exists inside today's modern stadium. (AF-P6150 [45] [015].)

Bohn Hilliard making touchdown that defeated Notre Dame Oct 6th 1934 in Notre Dame Stadium. Final score Texas U 7 Notre Dame 6.

This 1934 photograph shows Bohn Hilliard scoring a touchdown against Notre Dame on October 6, 1934. UT won the game 7-6. This victory was relished, as Notre Dame has proven to be a tough competitor over the past 100 years. (C10047.)

This 1924 aerial view shows the UT Longhorn Band on the field, forming a giant "T," at Memorial Stadium's dedication. Another old tradition had band members remain in the stands and play while fans left their seats to perform a "snake dance," running single file up and down the length of the field to show support for the team. (C09993.)

This memorial is on the north side of Memorial Stadium. When the stadium was built, the student body dedicated it in honor of the 198,520 Texans—5,280 of whom lost their lives—fighting in World War I. On November 12, 1977, during the Texas Christian University–University of Texas game, a small granite monument was unveiled and placed at the base of the statue. The ceremony rededicated Texas Memorial Stadium to the memory of all alumni who participated in any American war. (Author's collection.)

Anna Hiss Gymnasium was built in 1931 as the women's gymnasium. In 1974, this gym, with its exquisite architecture and winsome interior spaces, was named after the former director of physical training for women, who served from 1921 to 1956. Over the course of 10 years, Hiss spent her own money touring gymnasiums across the country to compile ideas and plans, which she then used to assist the building's architects and to convince the university to fund the building. Hiss also helped found the women's intramural sports programs at UT, and cofounded the Orange Jackets. (C07572.)

The 1932 Longhorn Band is posing in front of Gregory Gym. Thomas Watt Gregory was one of the first 13 graduates of the University of Texas, having received his law degree in 1885. He later became attorney general under Woodrow Wilson. His fundraising efforts, supplemented by university funding, made possible today's Gregory Gym, Anna Hiss Gym, and the Texas Union Building. Gregory Gym served as the home for the UT basketball and swim teams until the 1970s. The original student-led varsity band, founded in 1900, purchased $150 worth of instruments from a local pawn shop and recruited 16 students to make up the band. From that modest start, it grew over the years and eventually earned the reputation of "Show Band of the Southwest." (PICA 28567.)

Gregory Gym is decorated for Franklin D. Roosevelt's birthday in 1934. Built in 1931, it was used as an auditorium and gymnasium. In the years before the Frank Erwin Center, students registered for classes at Gregory Gym; in late August, they would have to stand in long, hot lines that started outside. (PICA 25652.)

Kirby Hall Dormitory, shown in 2018, was built in 1924. The dorm was named after Helen M. Kirby, who in the 1880s became a supervisor of young women at the new university. In 1903, Kirby was named dean of women, a title she retained until her retirement in 1919. In 1976, it became the kindergarten-through-twelfth-grade private school Kirby Hall. (Author's collection.)

Scottish Rite Dormitory on West Twenty-Seventh street has been a women's dormitory since 1922. It is situated on seven acres one block north of campus and is still used for its intended purpose today. (Author's collection.)

Eastwoods Park is a shady nine-acre neighborhood park that sits along Waller Creek just north of the University of Texas. Prior to its development as a city park in 1930, Eastwoods was referred to as Wheeler's Grove. This park is also historically significant for hosting one of the earliest Juneteenth celebrations. Eastwoods has been a popular place for law school student gatherings and other student events, such as Eeyore's Birthday Party. (Author's collection.)

The Burleson Bells are part of a monument just outside Bass Concert Hall. The bells were donated by Albert Sidney Burleson in 1929 and were used in Old Main from 1930 to 1934. Burleson was an 1884 graduate of the law school and later served as US postmaster general. The bells were installed in this monument in 1981. (Author's collection.)

The Santa Rita No. 1 oil well was established on land set aside to support the two primary state universities, the University of Texas and Texas A&M. Fortunately, the land produced petroleum, and oil revenue dramatically changed the finances and, ultimately, the architectural landscape of UT. Stately buildings replaced the old shacks that had been necessary for the burgeoning student population in earlier years. This relic from the well can be seen at the corner of MLK Boulevard and Trinity Street in Austin. (PICA 07935.)

W.J. Battle joined the faculty as a professor of Greek and classical studies in 1893 and was highly respected on the Forty Acres. He served as UT president from 1914 to 1916 and is credited with designing the university seal and his instrumental role in founding the University Co-op. He is pictured in his study in Main Building around 1933. (PICB 03321.)

UT president Homer P. Rainey is shown here at a meeting on January 9, 1940. Rainey served as president from 1939 to 1944. Controversy surrounded him when the board of regents pressured him to fire a few professors over differing politics. The board also weakened tenure and cut funding for social science, both of which Rainey protested. This political divisiveness, along with Rainey's public protests and his effort to move the medical branch from Galveston to Austin a couple years earlier, led to his termination on November 1, 1944. After Rainey was fired, approximately 8,000 students marched in protest at the university and the state capitol. (PICB 12002.)

Former university president S.E. Mezes, along with other past presidents, is memorialized at Texas Union. Mezes, from California, was the son of a Spanish-born forty-niner. Mezes came to Austin as an adjunct professor of philosophy in 1898 and quickly advanced through the ranks, becoming the fifth university president. In his six years as president, the university added the Department of Extension, the Bureau of Economic Geology, and a new library. (Author's collection.)

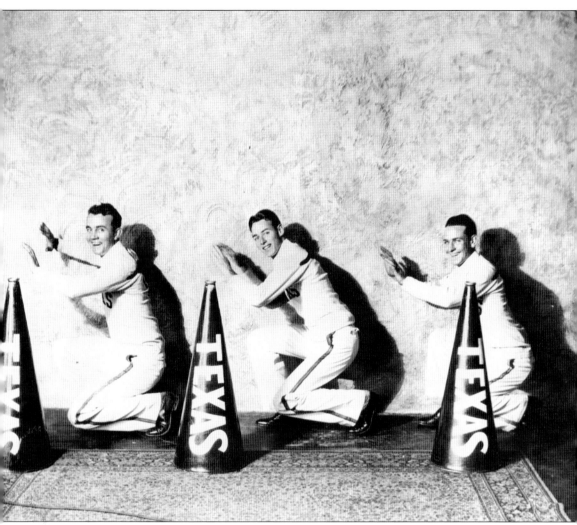

This undated photograph shows some University of Texas cheerleaders. A couple of well-known former cheerleaders are Harley Clark, who invented the hook 'em horns hand signal, and Neal Spelce, who led pep rallies atop Dirty Martin's KumBak Place during his days cheering for UT. Historically, boosting spirit for upcoming games has involved signs hung at the Texas Union, impromptu rallies in front of Hill Hall (later expanded to Moore-Hill), the residence for most of the athletes, and the red candle tradition, first employed in 1941 against the Aggies. In past years, candles burned brightly in store windows along the Drag, in offices downtown, and all over Austin. (PICA 17321.)

The university's School of Business Administration was founded in 1922. One of the most interesting features on display in the business school is this wooden remnant of the old New York Stock Exchange. Now ensconced in the McCombs School of Business, its acquisition was made possible by donations from various Texas companies. UT's business school has long held a great reputation and had to start limiting enrollment in the 1970s, when demand far exceeded supply. (Author's collection.)

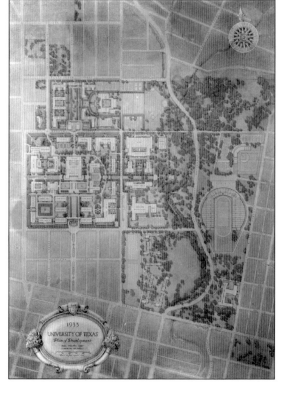

This 1933 plan for the University of Texas shows several future buildings. It also depicts existing structures, such as Littlefield Hall; Home Economics, Biology, Physics, Chemistry, Engineering, and Architecture buildings; Waggener Hall; the tower/library; Hogg Memorial Auditorium; Sutton and Garrison Halls; the museum, University Junior High School, and Gregory Gym. Clark Field can be seen just north of Memorial Stadium. (PICA 19506.)

This tree-lined water feature is known today as the Turtle Pond. Adjacent to the greenhouse, it was built between 1934 and 1939. The College of Natural Sciences oversees its upkeep. The pond holds a variety of turtle species. (Author's collection.)

Painter Hall, then the Physics Building, is shown here to the right of the pond. The domed observatory can be seen on the right. Built in 1933, it was renamed after geneticist T.S. Painter, who was UT president from 1944 to 1952. Painter is also known in US history as the respondent in the landmark Sweatt v. Painter civil rights case. (C06777.)

In 1927, Guadalupe Street was rather quiet compared to today. This section of the street, located near the university, is known as "the Drag." The Texas Bookstore, the University Co-op, a streetcar, and a pharmacy are seen in this photograph. (PICA 02251.)

Pictured in 1930 is Dirty Martin's KumBak Place at Twenty-Eighth and Guadalupe Streets. This restaurant, close to campus, has been a favorite destination for students and alumni since 1926. Cheerleaders used to host pep rallies from atop the roof while students gathered in the parking lot below. In years past, it was common for the university's athletic victories to be celebrated both on campus as well as in other areas of Austin, including downtown. (AR.2013.029 [163].)

Three

1940–1960

The mid-century period was marked by the war effort at the university as well as postwar changes at UT and across the city of Austin due to World War II. The university responded patriotically during the war, and it experienced enormous growth in its student population following the conflict. There was an effort to put up more classroom buildings and dormitories. Some private dormitories were added to the residential choices for students. The UT Defense Lab, which started with World War II, provided research and development, and eventually, the facilities led to the Applied Research Laboratories. The UT president and others believed World War II could be won with people who knew engineering and science. World War II was a broader war than past wars, and every part of civilian life was affected. The university also became a center of the civilian war effort. Classes were held on bandage-rolling and first aid. A recruitment center opened in the Texas Union Building. In the postwar years, UT acquired the George Washington sculpture that stands on the South Mall and was donated by the Daughters of the American Revolution. Several notable former students went on to long and distinguished careers during the postwar years. Heman Sweatt made headlines for trying to join the UT law school. Former student body president Mac Wallace made headlines for murder charges. Prominent educators from these years include such luminaries as Dr. W.J. Battle, Dr. George Isidore Sanchez, Dr. Carlos E. Castañeda, Dr. Américo Paredes, Carl Eckhardt, and J. Frank Dobie.

Aerial View of the University of Texas, Austin, Texas   OB-H533

The Growth of UT quickly accelerated after World War II. This postcard aerial view shows the postwar campus with some key buildings identified: 1. Sutton Hall, 2. Architectural Building, 3. Texas Union, 4. Woman's Building, 5. Hogg Auditorium, 6. Biology Building, 7. Home Economics Building, 8. Andrews Hall, 9. Carothers Hall, 10. Littlefield Hall, 11. University Methodist Church, 12. School of Fine Arts (Littlefield House), 13. Grace Hall, 14. Scottish Rite Dormitory, 15. Administration Building, 16. Physics Building, 17. Chemistry Building, 18. Women's Gymnasium, 19. Engineering Building, 20. Journalism Building, 21. Geology Building, 22. Garrison Hall, 23. Waggener Hall, 24. Law Building, 25. Gregory Gym, and 26. Littlefield Memorial Fountain. (AF-P6150 [45] [009].)

The Gordon-White Building has been used by the College of Liberal Arts since 1951. Above one of the building's entrances is carved "Vincit Omnia Veritas," or "Truth Conquers all Things." The building is used today for African diaspora studies and Mexican American and Latino/Latina studies. (Authors collection.)

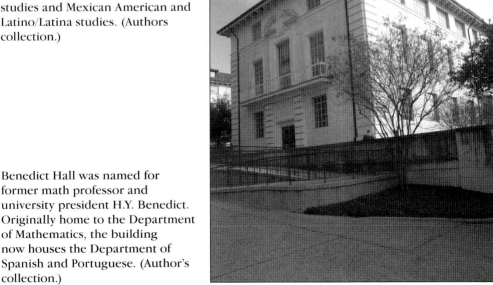

Benedict Hall was named for former math professor and university president H.Y. Benedict. Originally home to the Department of Mathematics, the building now houses the Department of Spanish and Portuguese. (Author's collection.)

Rainey Hall, formerly the Music Building, was erected along the South Mall, and is named for former university president Homer Rainey. It is one of six buildings that comprise what is commonly called "the Six Pack." Flanking the South Mall, these buildings are Rainey Hall (1941) Calhoun Hall (1967), Parlin Hall (1955), Batts Hall (1951), Mezes Hall (1951), and Benedict Hall (1951). (Author's collection.)

Two men are pictured in front of the International Center and International Office in Wooldridge Hall in 1959. Wooldridge Hall was originally built as an elementary school and was acquired by UT in 1966. It was on Twenty-Fourth Street between Nueces and Seton Streets and was demolished in 2010. (ND-59-4871-03.)

Kinsolving Hall, a dormitory, was built in 1958 and named after the Episcopal bishop of the Diocese of Texas, Rt. Rev. George H. Kinsolving, whose house once sat on the same spot. During the university's rocky history of integration, many protests, speeches, and sit-ins were held at Kinsolving. In 1964, UT announced that it would integrate all residence halls on campus. (Author's collection.)

Moore-Hill Dormitory provided living space for student athletes before Jester Dormitory was built. Moore-Hill was formed by joining Hill Dormitory (1939) and Moore Dormitory (1955). They are named for Dr. Homer B. Hill of Austin, who volunteered to treat the UT football team from the very first game in 1893 until his death in 1923, and for Victor I. Moore, who served as dean of student life from 1927 to 1943. (Author's collection.)

The A-Bar Hotel was a private men's dormitory at 2612 Guadalupe Street, shown here in 1949 when it was new. This view is from the Twenty-Seventh Street side. Years later, this became Taos Cooperative. Today, the building shows its age but is still recognizable. (ND-49-543-06.)

Among the ever-changing storefronts on Guadalupe Street, the Goodall Wooten dormitory has remained a constant for 62 years. It opened as an upscale student dormitory; however, in 2018, it was fatigued, and residents were given short notice just before it closed. (Author's collection.)

Smokey the Cannon, also known as Old Smokey, is brought to UT football games and is managed by a student service organization known as the Texas Cowboys. The group was created by the mechanical engineering lab in 1953 in response to shotgun blasts often heard during the Red River Rivalry with Oklahoma. There have been different cannons used over the years. The current version, Smokey III, is a replica Civil War artillery piece that weighs over 1,200 pounds. (Author's collection.)

Hook 'Em Horns

This is hook 'em horns, the University of Texas Longhorns hand signal. The word "horns," short for Longhorns, has come to refer to university teams. Head yell leader Harley Clark introduced it to boost audience participation during games. Classmate Henry "HK" Pitts had previously suggested that the hand sign, with the index and little fingers extended, looked a bit like horns, and might be fun to do at rallies and football games. So, in 1955, Clark introduced it at a Gregory Gym rally. The hand signal quickly became a cherished tradition with fans. (Lauren Duran.)

Big Bertha, the eight-foot-tall UT Longhorn Band drum, is pictured in 1959. The basketball player on the left is Alberto Almanza, and the band member on the right is Pat Carpenter. Bertha was created at the University of Chicago and began its career there, but when the school dropped varsity football in 1939, Harold Byrd, a benefactor of the Longhorn Band, recommended that the drum be purchased. Moton Crockett, former director of the Longhorn Band, purchased Bertha for $1 and transported the drum from Elkhart, Indiana, to Austin. Crockett refurbished the drum, and Big Bertha became a special member of the Longhorn Band in 1955. Bertha is a focal point at public appearances. (Prints and Photographs Collection, the Dolph Briscoe Center for American History, the University of Texas at Austin.)

TEXAS LONGHORNS OF 1941
AND BIG BOY THEIR MASCOT

Pictured are the 1941 football players and "Big Boy," their longhorn mascot. This team had a great season and was ranked No. 1 in the Associated Press poll. Though they were not selected to play in the Rose Bowl, but they did make the cover of *Life* magazine. The idea of using a live longhorn as the university's mascot is attributed to UT alumnus Stephen Pinckney in 1916. The first time a longhorn joined the UT football team on the field was in 1916. Next, a Hereford named Bevo II joined the team in 1936, and Bevo III came along in 1945. Since then, longhorns have been used with regularity, replaced as they aged or due to temperament. Not all of the Bevos responded well to the enthusiasm and energy of the football games. Other teams have been known to saw off Bevo's horns (University of Oklahoma) or kidnap Bevo (Texas A&M), so they are heavily guarded. Many of the past Bevos come from the same bloodline. A dog named Pig Belmont was an unofficial mascot in 1914. The dog was a popular fixture on campus, but he died when hit by a car in 1923. Bevo carried on as the lone mascot. (PICA 19649.)

Pictured is a Defense Research Lab in 1946. UT's role in defense research started in 1942, during World War II, with the production of magnesium. The university has been involved in federal projects ever since. During World War II, the federal government partnered with universities to gain access to experts in engineering and science. UT professors signed up for service, and vital fields for the war effort became the focus of the university. Instruction was extended over the entire year, and engineering labs were running 24 hours. UT scientists worked on the atomic bomb and a number of other critical projects. The university was also turning out naval midshipmen as part of the V-12 Navy College Training Program. Today, Applied Research Laboratories is a US Department of Defense university research center. Since 1945, it has been engaged in sponsored research dedicated to improving national security through applications of science. (C06977.)

This 1954 photograph shows the Texas Memorial Museum and the *Mustangs* sculpture in front. Built in 1937, the Texas Memorial Museum is the university's museum for natural science and Texas history, created during preparations for the Texas Centennial Exposition in 1936. (ND-54-517-01.)

Ralph Ogden, an Austin oilman and cattleman, donated money to secure *Mustangs* for the university. A. Phiminster Proctor, recommended by Frank Dobie, was selected to create the sculpture. The bronze work was unveiled at commencement exercises in 1948. (Author's collection.)

With the 200th anniversary of George Washington's birth coming up in 1932, the UT regents unanimously approved the idea of a monument honoring his memory, and invited the Daughters of the American Revolution to place a monument on campus. The goal was to unveil the sculpture in 1932, but due to inadequate funds and other issues, it took many more years to complete. After World War II, the economy improved, and interest in the statue grew. Enough money was collected, and Pompeo Coppini, the Italian-born sculptor who produced the university's Littlefield Memorial Fountain, was recruited to add one more sculpture to UT's collection, which was placed on the South Mall in 1955. (Author's collection.)

Dr. W.J. Battle had an amazingly long career at UT. He started in 1893 as a professor of classical languages, and for the next 55 years continued in various positions, including as president from 1914 to 1916. Battle was involved in the designing of the UT seal and founding the University Co-op. He chaired the faculty building committee from 1920 to 1948. The design of the campus and its buildings were carefully selected for Texas weather. Battle is shown here about the time he retired, in 1948. (ND-49-322-01.)

Dr. George Isidore Sanchez was a UT educator from 1940 until his death in 1972. Sanchez served the university as a professor in the Department of History and Philosophy of Education, as well as a consultant in Latin American education. He was also a civil rights leader and had a positive influence on the acceptance of bilingual education and preschool education. (PICB 11735.)

Heman Marion Sweatt is shown at the registration office. Sweatt was well prepared for law school when he applied to the University of Texas School of Law in 1946. Though qualified, he was denied admission due to his race. Sweatt filed a lawsuit citing that denying him admission was an infringement of his rights under the Fourteenth Amendment of the US Constitution. The university tried setting up separate law school classes, but the case went to the US Supreme Court. In 1950, the court decided in Sweatt's favor, stating that separate educational opportunities were not equal and that equal protection under the Fourteenth Amendment required that Sweatt be admitted. Following his historic win, UT opened its graduate courses to all qualified black students. (ND-50-283-02.)

Dr. Carlos E. Castañeda was a noted professor of Latin American history and librarian of the Latin American Collection at the university. Castañeda's work as a historian focused on the Spanish borderlands, especially Texas. UT honored both him and Dr. Ervin Perry by naming the new library after them. (ND-49-191-01.)

Dr. Américo Paredes taught folklore and creative writing at UT. Paredes's own writings often focused on the border life between the United States and Mexico. In 1958, the University of Texas Press published his dissertation as a book, *With His Pistol in His Hand: A Border Ballad and Its Hero*. Paredes is a world-renowned scholar of Mexican American studies, folklore, and the US-Mexico borderlands and was instrumental in the founding of the Center for Mexican American Studies at UT. (PICB 17506.)

Charismatic student body president Malcolm E. "Mac" Wallace is speaking to students on campus in 1944 during the Homer Rainey controversy. Wallace led a student protest against the firing of university president Homer Rainey. Wallace's time as president of the student body may have been the high point of his life. He went on to a career in government, defense contracting, and private industry, but his future was tarnished by his own criminal actions and rumored nefarious political undertakings for Pres. Lyndon Johnson. (ND-44-123a-03.)

Just seven years after being a student leader at UT, Mac Wallace (left) is shown here at his bond hearing for the murder of Austin golf pro Douglas Kinser in 1951. Wallace was working as an economist with the US Department of Agriculture in Washington, DC, when in October 1951, he visited Austin and shot Kinser, presumably over Kinser's involvement with Wallace's wife. Wallace was arrested shortly afterwards, tried, found guilty, and sentenced to a five-year prison term that was suspended. (ND-51-175a-01.)

Ralph Yarborough is pictured at his desk in 1952 when he challenged the incumbent governor of Texas but lost the election. After graduating from the University of Texas School of Law in 1927, Yarborough became a prominent Texas Democratic politician. He served in the US Senate from 1957 to 1971 and was a leader of the progressive wing of his party. (ND-52-139-01.)

Texas governor Daniel Moody, shown here in 1942, was a distinguished UT law school graduate. Moody served as governor of Texas from 1927 to 1931 and was credited with the prosecution of the Ku Klux Klan in Texas and with restoring integrity to state government. (ND-42-136-02.)

Carl Eckhardt is shown in 1949. Eckhardt taught mechanical engineering at the university from 1936 until his retirement in 1973. At the same time, he served as superintendent of the university's power plant from 1930 to 1937, superintendent of utilities from 1937 to 1950, and director of the physical plant from 1950 to 1970. Eckhardt was also a historian who wrote six books about UT Austin. He planted numerous trees along Waller Creek and is credited with starting one of the greatest traditions at UT, the orange lighting of the tower. Eckhardt's orange lights first flooded the tower in 1937. In 1947, he helped create guidelines for using the lights. (ND-49-339-01.)

US Supreme Court chief justice Tom C. Clark is shown in 1950. Clark received his law degree from the University of Texas in 1922. Pres. Harry Truman appointed him US attorney general in 1945 and to the Supreme Court in 1949. He was the first Texan to serve on the Supreme Court. (ND-50-181-04.)

J. Frank Dobie, seen here in 1943, was an American folklorist, newspaper columnist, and prolific writer, best known for his books about life in Texas. Dobie came to Austin in 1914 to teach at the University of Texas and developed a self-styled class named Life and Literature of the Southwest. In his book *The Forty-Acre Follies*, Joe B. Frantz said, "Whatever else he was, Dobie was Texas's first liberated mind to achieve a wide audience, and the first truly professional writer produced by the state." Dobie was a progressive activist whose vocal politics led to his leaving the university in 1947. But he continued writing until his death in 1964, publishing over 25 books and countless articles. The university has maintained a large collection of Dobie's writings. (ND-43-120-04.)

John B. Connally is shown in 1947 when he served as an aide to Sen. Lyndon B. Johnson. Connally had graduated from the UT School of Law in 1941 and served in World War II. After the war, he was recruited to become an aide to Johnson. Connally later served as governor of Texas from 1963 to 1969. In 1963, as governor, he rode in the presidential limousine during President Kennedy's assassination and was seriously wounded. (ND-47-152-01.)

This 1952 view of the Drag includes the Varsity Theatre in the foreground on the right and campus on the left. The lack of traffic compared to today is noticeable. Opened in 1936, the Varsity's first movie was the black-and-white Western *The Texas Rangers*. In 1979, the building received a makeover with a mural of the history of movies on the Twenty-Fourth Street side of the building. The theater played its last film and shut its doors in 1990. (PICA 26827.)

In 1951, the Texas Bookstore and the University Co-op sat side by side on the Drag directly across from Texas Union. The University Co-op was originally located inside Main Building when its mission was to provide students with their books and supplies. Twenty-two years after it was founded on campus, the Co-op moved to the Drag. (ND-51-169-02.)

This 1950s photograph shows the Night Hawk restaurant, which featured late-night hours when that was a rarity in Austin. Night Hawk was an instant hit with UT faculty and students, becoming a neighborhood hangout for generations. The university crowd ate, studied, courted, and celebrated there. But over time, fast food and other restaurants moved into the university area, and in 1980, the Night Hawk closed. (PICA 09547.)

Four

1960–1969

The 1960s brought a lot of excitement to the university, and most, but not all, of it was the good kind. UT built the largest student residential building in the United States. This period also saw the rise of other buildings, such as the Forty Acres Club, which President Johnson casually integrated one day; the Music Building & Recital Hall; Academic Center; the Texas Exes Building; and the Communications Building, which broadcasted *Austin City Limits* and other programs. But the University Junior High School came to an end. That joint effort between the local school district and the University of Texas had been successful, but UT was growing again, so the junior high building was repurposed. One of UT's most famous and controversial regent board members, Frank Erwin, wielded his power while adeptly guiding the university through some turbulent times. Sadly, UT student Charles Whitman went to the top of Main Building's tower and shot people below. A former UT law school graduate, John Connally, became governor. Other students, such as Farrah Fawcett and Janis Joplin, became famous entertainers. Darrell Royal was in the middle of his outstanding career, building UT's famed football program. The University of Texas gained a national presence by the end of the decade. Student traditions and service operations like the Silver Spurs and the Greek system continued to thrive. Other traditions, like "running the flag" and Eeyore's Birthday Party, got their start. And by the end of the 1960s, the nationwide youth counterculture movement attracted and influenced students here.

Walter Webb Hall, shown here today, originally held the Forty Acres Club, which opened in 1962. The club was the scene of social events and operated as a luxury hotel. Pres. Lyndon Johnson integrated the Forty Acres in 1963 when he escorted Gerri Wittington, an African American and one of his personal secretaries in the White House, to an event at the club. The university bought the club in 1972 and later named it Walter Webb Hall after the historian and author. (Author's collection.)

Newman Hall opened in 1969 as a dormitory for Catholic women. It is across from the Dobie Center residence hall. St. Austin's Parish has been active in the university area since 1908. (Author's collection.)

UT's Jester Center Residence Halls were built in 1969 to house almost 3,000 students. The size required a separate zip code. Some alumni recall hijinks at Jester, such as panty raids and jock raids in the 1970s. This complex was UT's first step into coed dormitories. Jester is named after former student and UT regent Beauford H. Jester, who served Texas as governor from 1947 to 1949. (Author's collection.)

UT's new buildings in the late 1960s included the Music Building & Recital Hall, which opened by 1969 to house the voice, woodwind, brass, string, and percussion faculty; the Longhorn Band; choral organizations; the university's symphony orchestra; and the university's symphonic band. (Author's collection.)

Frank Erwin attended UT law school. Later, he served as a regent for the university from 1963 to 1975 and was chairman of the board from 1966 to 1971. Erwin had a controversial reputation when dealing with the burgeoning counterculture movement of the late 1960s and early 1970s. He also tried to move the stadium to north of Forty-Fifth Street, but Darrell Royal and others prevented that. His legacy includes Disch-Falk baseball stadium, an enlarged Memorial Stadium, the Texas Swimming Center, the Special Events Center (later renamed after him), the fountain facing Sid Richardson Hall, the complex of buildings to the east of Interstate 35, and the azaleas and stone fences around some of the campus's edges. (UT News and Information Services, Prints and Photographs Collection, the Dolph Briscoe Center for American History, the University of Texas at Austin.)

The Etter-Harbin Alumni Center was built in 1965 and extensively renovated in the 1980s. Located across the street from the football stadium, the alumni association, known as the "Texas Exes," has been in existence since the first class of students graduated in 1885. It was formed that year to help maintain contact with students after they left the Forty Acres. (Author's collection.)

This postcard shows Memorial Stadium and campus buildings in the 1960s. With coach Darrell Royal and great football players, the Longhorns won three national championships in 1963, 1969, and 1970, and 11 Southwest Conference titles. Royal's teams also gave college football the wishbone defense. Students could use the track at Memorial Stadium when it was not being used by student athletes. To get tickets for football games, many Alumni remember having to wait in overnight lines, which turned into parties. (AF-P6150 [45] [013].)

Along Guadalupe Street this School of Communication building is where *Austin City Limits* was originally produced and televised. In 1974, Willie Nelson agreed to perform at Studio 6A, and this eventually led to the first broadcast of the show in 1976. (Author's collection.)

The Academic Center, providing study spaces and computer labs, was built in 1963 and, years later, was named after UT president Peter Flawn. Flawn had been a geology professor in the 1960s and then served as vice president of academic affairs. He presided over the university's centennial celebration in 1983, and served as UT president from 1979 to 1985 and as ad interim president from 1997 to 1998. The Academic Center is where the Woman's Building was once located. (Author's collection.)

Pictured in 1967 is the Engineering-Science Building with a pool. The university has one of the world's highest ranked and most respected engineering schools, established in 1900. Within 10 years, it had branched out to include departments for civil, mining, electrical, mechanical, and chemical engineering. Alumnus Rob Oliver recalls that in the 1970s, engineering students would prepare their software programs on punch cards and submit them to be read at the Computation Center, in an underground building below East Mall's stairs. (ASPL_DM-67-32628.)

Pictured in 1967 is the six-story Engineering-Science Building. Within the first 100 years of the university, engineering had gone from a single classroom for its mostly rural and small-town students to a well-respected program with multiple disciplines and buildings, attracting students from all over the world. (ASPL_DM-67-32626.)

THE DAILY TEXAN

SERVING THE UNIVERSITY OF TEXAS AT AUSTIN COMMUNITY SINCE 1900

@THEDAILYTEXAN | THEDAILYTEXAN.COM   FRIDAY, AUGUST 23, 2019   FALL 2019

NEWS

MOOOV-IN EDITION

UT to provide free tuition to families earning up to $65,000

By Nicole Stuessy
PUBLISHED ON JULY 9, 2019

Starting in the fall of 2020, in-state undergraduate students who come from families with yearly incomes of up to $65,000 will...

The *Daily Texan* has been UT's student newspaper since 1900 and is still in publication. It has proved to be a springboard for the careers of a host of notable journalists, such as Walter Cronkite, Bill Moyers, and Liz Smith, and cartoonists like Berke Breathed and Ben Sargent. Other noteworthy *Daily Texan* alumni include Lady Bird Johnson and Liz Carpenter. (Author's collection.)

This photograph shows a puff of smoke during the time engineering student Charles Whitman was shooting from the tower. Shortly before noon on August 1, 1966, Whitman boarded an elevator to the observation deck carrying an arsenal of weapons. He shot at victims on the ground below for approximately 96 minutes until he was killed by Austin police officers. Whitman had killed his mother and his wife earlier that day. Sixteen people died that day, and more than 30 were wounded. (PICA 37423.)

This photograph was taken from the observation deck following the Charles Whitman shooting. The lower density of development looks refreshingly less congested compared to the crowded landscape today. (PICA 37429.)

Holding a guitar and cigarette, Janis Joplin is shown in 1963 at the Wednesday night Chuckwagon folk singing. The young man to her right is presumed to be Kirk Lanier Wiggins. Joplin grew up in Port Arthur, Texas, and came to the University of Texas in 1962 to study art. She found counterculture soulmates at "the Ghetto," a small apartment building near the university, and involved herself in music performances around Austin, including Kenneth Threadgill's beer joint. Threadgill's place was a converted filling station and late-night hangout for music lovers. Joplin became a world-famous rock and roll star before dying in 1970 from a drug overdose. (The Dolph Briscoe Center for American History, the University of Texas at Austin.)

The 10 most beautiful women on campus were pictured in the 1965–1966 *Cactus*. They are identified as Violantha June Ricks, Marsha Gay Gostecnick, Anne Sewell, Paula B. Savage, Sherry Spardley, Donna Raye Morton, Martha Kuhl, Nancy Lynn Haralson, Farrah Leni Fawcett, and Marcia Ruth Lucas. Farrah Fawcett, at center in the back row, left the university before graduating and went on to become a television and movie celebrity. (Dolph Briscoe Center for American History, the University of Texas at Austin.)

Eeyore's Birthday Party began in the spring of 1964 as a party and picnic hosted by Plan II students and faculty. Named for the chronically depressed donkey in A.A. Milne's Winnie-the-Pooh stories, the original event featured a trashcan full of lemonade, beer, honey sandwiches, a flower-draped donkey, and a May pole. For many years, the party was a tradition at Eastwoods Park. Early attendees recall that it was more family-friendly prior to its 1974 move to Pease District Park. (PICA 13051.)

Longhorn Band members are running the flag during a 1965 game against Texas Tech. The first flag measured 51 feet by 90 feet and was given to Texas governor Price Daniel by Mississippi governor Ross Barnett at the Cotton Bowl in 1962. But it was made of muslin and disintegrated within five years. In the 1970s, nylon was used and was more durable. The fans loved the flag running, so new flags were made as needed, and the tradition continued. Alpha Phi Omega has carried the flag across the field during halftime in football games, and it is hauled in its own trailer for away games. (C07254.)

The *Family Group* sculpture, created by lauded UT sculptor and educator Charles Umlauf, was designed in 1962 and placed in front of the Business School. At the base of the sculpture, there is a plaque that reads, "The family is the foundation upon which the world of business is built, and it is a vital force in the local, state and national economy." (Author's collection.)

Frank Dobie, the prolific Texas writer and former UT educator, lived in this house just north of the university along what is now Dean Keeton Street. This was his house along Waller Creek that he mentioned in his book prefaces. Dobie died in 1964, and his house has since become the James A. Michener Center for Writers. (Author's collection.)

In 1962, Charles Umlauf created the *Torchbearers* bronze sculpture. Umlauf was a longtime UT fine arts professor and was also known for being the sculpture mentor to student Farrah Fawcett. *Torchbearers* was installed outside the Academic Center and has been described as representing remarkable athletic ability or the passing of knowledge from teachers to students. (Author's collection.)

John and Nellie Connally give the hook 'em horns sign at an event on the day of Lyndon Johnson's presidential election. Some 23 years earlier, John was an outstanding student at UT, and Nellie Connally was named Sweetheart of the University in 1938. (ND-64-a001-04.)

Perhaps Austin's most unusual junior high school, which was the product of a joint effort between UT and the City of Austin, is pictured here. The school opened in September 1933 with an enrollment of 831 in the sixth through eighth grades. It provided the university's education department the opportunity to observe, demonstrate, and explore educational theories. It also provided Austin with another much-needed junior high. The agreement stipulated that UT would provide the site, building, and furnishings. (The Texas Historical Commission.)

The University Junior High School entrance is pictured. Austin Public Schools selected and paid the regular teaching staff and half the salary of the principal. UT's growth precipitated the school's closure in June 1967, and since then, this building has hosted the university's School of Social Work. (The Texas Historical Commission.)

Pictured in 1967 are Alpha Xi Delta sorority members. The UT chapter of this sorority was founded in 1929. The first sororities at UT may have been Kappa Kappa Gamma and Pi Beta Phi, which both opened in 1902. UT yearbooks from the first 100 years have numerous photographs of sorority leaders and campus sweethearts. (ND-67-423-01.)

Some UT Silver Spurs members are seen here facing the Littlefield Memorial Fountain and University of Texas Tower in 1965. Founded in 1937, the Silver Spurs is an honorary student service organization responsible for the care and transportation of Bevo, the university's longhorn mascot. In 1963, the Spurs worked with the Texas Rangers to find Bevo after he was kidnapped by Texas A&M students. Bevo was returned—unharmed—in time for the football game with the Aggies, and Texas won the game. (ND-65-232-02.)

By the late 1960s, things were changing. This 1968 photograph, taken by Forrest Preece, shows a love-in at Austin's Wooldridge Park. More than a few UT students participated, and the campus was certainly not isolated from the cultural changes taking place across the country. But in the university yearbook that year, the great majority of students are still dressed conservatively and neatly, with perfectly styled hair. (Forrest Preece.)

Texas psychedelic band Shiva's Headband, led by Spencer Perskins, is playing at the same 1968 love-in. Some alumni from this time recall seeing the band play at the Vulcan Gas Company nightclub at 316 Congress Avenue. The Vulcan opened in 1966 and was likely the first psychedelic club in Texas. It hosted both national and local acts but lasted only four years before closing. The band's drummer, Jerry Barnett, had been in UT's Longhorn Band along with Forrest Preece. (Forrest Preece.)

Five

1970–1983

During these 13 years, the UT campus acquired large, modern buildings such as the Frank Erwin Center, Dobie Dormitory, the Harry Ransom Center, Belmont Hall, Bass Concert Hall, the UT College of Education, the Texas Swim Center, Bauer Hose, the Perry Castañeda Library, Sid Richardson Hall, and the Jesse H. Jones Building. The university also was selected for the site of the Lyndon Baines Johnson Presidential Library. Barbara Jordan was recognized when a sculpture of hers was added to the historic Battle Oaks ground on campus. Famed sports legends, such as James Street and Earl Campbell, left their larger-than-life imprints on the university. In the mid-1970s, Darrell Royal retired as UT's very successful football coach; however, he never completely left the university after retirement. As for earlier acclaimed baseball coaches, Billy Disch and Bibb Falk were honored when the new baseball field was named after them. Meanwhile, some students were active in protesting the escalating war in southeast Asia and UT's involvement in that war, while protests were going on at the same time at other colleges nationwide. Both the Silver Spurs and the Longhorn Band grew in prominence. Spring Round-Up festivities, which had once been supported by a wider community, became the domain of the Greek system. Finally, a number of private enterprises became important commercial outlets for students and long-standing memories for alumni.

The LBJ Library was the first presidential library placed on a university campus. Lady Bird Johnson is credited with suggesting this placement. It was dedicated in 1971 with LBJ and President Nixon in attendance. The library is grand, and the fifth floor looks especially elegant with rows and shelves holding mandarin-red boxes that contain historical documents related to the Johnson presidency. The library sits adjacent to the Lyndon B. Johnson School of Public Affairs. (Author's collection.)

The Frank Erwin Center opened in 1977 and was originally known as the Special Events Center, or the Superdrum, due to its appearance. The facility has hosted entertainment events, and has been home court for the men's and women's basketball programs. Adjacent to downtown Austin, the Erwin Center is a premier venue for large events, both public and private. (Author's collection.)

Robert Lee Moore Hall, named for the longtime UT mathematician, dates to 1972 and is used for physics, mathematics, and astronomy. Dr. Moore graduated from UT in 1901 and then returned to teach from 1920 to 1969, when he was 86 years old. He was known for his leading work in general topology and for the Moore method of teaching university mathematics. But his standing has been tarnished by reports of his discrimination against minorities and women. (Author's collection.)

The 27-story Dobie Center dormitory and its retail center opened in 1972. The Dobie Center originally was clad with light-brown brick and was well positioned adjacent to the campus, with nice amenities and features. Named after J. Frank Dobie, the dorm is a privately owned residence hall. The Dobie had a facelift in 1990 and currently sports this glass exterior. (Author's collection.)

Approximately 450 miles west of Austin is UT's prominent McDonald Observatory, which debuted its *StarDate* radio program in 1978. The program is just one of the many contributions made to science at the observatory, one of the world's leading centers for astronomical research, teaching, and public education and outreach. The two large domes in the foreground are the Struve Telescope to the left and the Smith Telescope to the right. The Hobby-Eberly Telescope is at center in the distance. The observatory facilities are atop Mount Locke and Mount Fowlkes in the Davis Mountains of West Texas. (Damond Benningfield.)

The Harry Ransom Center opened in 1972. It acquires, preserves, and manages collections of significant cultural materials such as rare books, manuscripts, film, and art. It is named after Harry Ransom, a master collector who rose through the ranks at UT as a professor, dean, president, and chancellor. (Author's collection.)

In 1972, Bellmont Hall was added to Memorial Stadium to house intercollegiate athletics offices, physical education facilities, and lecture halls. It was named for L.T. Bellmont, UT athletic director from 1913 to 1957, who helped create Memorial Stadium and the Southwest Conference. Bellmont is remembered for scheduling UT to play Oklahoma at the annual Cotton Bowl game in Dallas. The rivalry is still enjoyed by fans on both sides. (Author's collection.)

Bass Concert Hall opened in 1981 on the site of what had previously been Clark Field with its havoc-creating limestone cliff in the outfield. This flagship theater of the Texas Performing Arts Center is a popular venue on campus. (Author's collection.)

The UT College of Education was founded in 1891 when it was called the School of Pedagogy. This modern building was constructed in 1975. Nearly 20 years later, it was renamed for George I. Sanchez, who had been an influential UT educator from 1940 until 1972. (Author's collection.)

Professor Ernest Lundelius, geologist and paleontologist, is pictured in Balcones Research Center in 1975. The 475-acre center is located in northwest Austin and is named for the Balcones Escarpment, which runs through it. After World War II, the former home of a magnesium plant became home to laboratories for scientists and engineers in civil, electronic, aerospace, mechanical, petroleum, and environmental-health engineering research, along with scientific research in botany, zoology, paleontology, nuclear physics, chemistry, psychology, atmospheric science, and archeology. It is now the J.J. Pickle Research Campus. (PICA 12466.)

An unidentified woman is seen working at the Balcones Research Center. UT has historically had facilities off the main campus. Offsite locations include the McDonald Observatory in the Davis Mountains, and the Brackenridge Field Laboratory along the Colorado River on land that was gifted to the university by George Brackenridge. (PICA 12467.)

James Street was a standout quarterback and baseball player who arrived at the University of Texas in 1966. As the operator of Darrell K. Royal's remarkable wishbone offense, Street led the Longhorns to a national championship in 1969. The Longhorns won the 1970 Cotton Bowl where well-known Longhorn Freddie Steinmark, who had just had one of his legs amputated due to cancer, watched his team beat Notre Dame from the sidelines. UT would go on to claim another national championship in 1970. (PICB 14144.)

Celebrated football coach Darrell Royal served as head coach from 1957 to 1976. During his time, the Longhorns never had a losing season. After they became national champions in 1963, a tradition was started with the University of Texas Tower bathed in orange lights and a No. 1 on all four sides. Royal led the Longhorns to two more national championships in 1969 and 1970. He was known for being a disciplined, brilliant coach with a great personality and folksy sayings like "We're gonna dance with who brung us." Today, Memorial Stadium has been renamed Darrell K. Royal–Texas Memorial Stadium. Royal elevated football at UT while he became a national celebrity as well as a friend to Willie Nelson and other famous people. (PICB 19943.)

Star football player Earl Campbell and Darrell Royal are shown during the retirement of Campbell's No. 20 jersey. Campbell became the first Texas Longhorn to win the Heisman Trophy after leading his team to an undefeated regular season in 1977. When he won the Heisman as a UT player in 1977, the entire length of the Drag was solidly packed with cars honking their horns. Students on campus gathered around the tower wearing whatever they happened to have on at the time, including pajamas and bathrobes, as it was announced late in the evening. Business owners in the UT area posted congratulations to Campbell on their marquees and storefronts. (PICB 10965.)

Fred Akers served as head football coach from 1977 to 1986. He had been assistant coach under Darrell Royal from 1966 to 1974. Under Akers, the Longhorns won two Southwest Conference titles in 1977 and 1983, and his record of 86-13-2 (60-19-1 in the SWC) is just behind Royal's on the all-time UT victory list. (PICB 18822.)

Disch-Falk Field (1975) is named after the university's legendary baseball coaches W.J. "Uncle Billy" Disch (1911–1939) and Bibb Falk (1940–1967). Together, they stacked up an impressive record of 989 wins and 357 losses. They also won 40 conference championships and two national championships. The field is near the university on the east side of I-35. (Prints and Photographs Collection, the Dolph Briscoe Center for American History, the University of Texas at Austin.)

Dr. Donald Goodall is pictured in Michener Art Gallery. Goodall was a professor of art history and a founding director of UT's Blanton Museum of Art. Starting in 1968, UT received hundreds of 20th-century American paintings and financial gifts from the esteemed novelist James A. Michener and his wife, Mari. (PICA 12435.)

Pictured is a parade during the 1977 Roundup. The annual spring celebration started in 1930 as a weekend of alumni reunions, campus expositions, open houses for UT departments, dances, and parades. The event once included more community involvement but has evolved into a campus event hosted by the UT Interfraternity Council. (PICA 12543.)

This stone carving of skulls at Chichen Itza in Mexico was photographed by the author in 1982. UT scholars David Stuart and Linda Schele had major roles in deciphering the Mayan hieroglyphics in the Yucatan and Central America. David Stuart, a professor of Mesoamerican art at UT, is considered an expert on Maya culture. Linda Schele produced a large number of important works on ancient Maya culture and founded the annual Maya Meetings at UT in the late 1970s. (Author's collection.)

The Texas Swim Center opened in 1977. Tex Robertson developed the swim team and was its head coach from 1936 to 1943 and again from 1946 to 1950. Robertson led the Longhorns to 13 Southwest Conference championships. In the 1990s, it was renamed after UT benefactors Lee and Joe Jamail. (Author's collection.)

Since chancellor Charles A. LeMaistre and his family moved into the Bauer House in 1971, the Tarrytown house has been the home for UT chancellors and their families. The stately home is the site of many official UT functions and is furnished and decorated with items from antique and art collections of the Harry Ransom Humanities Research Center and the Jack S. Blanton Museum of Art. (PICA 28520.)

In 1979, Barbara Jordan became a professor at the Lyndon B. Johnson School of Public Affairs at UT. Previously, she had held a long and distinguished political career in Congress, where she was known for her oratory and powerful vision. Through all of her work, Jordan was a champion of civil rights who worked tirelessly to create an inclusive and respectful society for all. (PICB 17608.)

The Barbara Jordan statue is surrounded by the Battle Oaks. A few live oak trees, hundreds of years old, remain adjacent to the student union. The Orange Jackets women's service organization is credited with the drive to erect the statue, the first of a female at UT. Most of the trees in the same grove were cut down in the early days of the Civil War. At that time, Union forces captured Galveston, and the trees were deemed obstructions to the construction of a fort that would protect Austin. While the fortress never materialized, the trees were lost forever. (Author's collection.)

Student protesters are seen marching on Congress Avenue with flags and signs. During the first week of May 1970, the largest protest in UT history occurred when students marched both on campus and in Austin streets to protest the war in Vietnam. With as many as 25,000 participants from the student body, this protest occurred after the Kent State killings. The activism and sometimes violent protests mirrored that at other college campuses. In the 1960s, protests had taken place over the university's institutionalized racial discrimination polices and student repression by the administration. (PICA 15667.)

These demonstrators are marching to Bauer House in 1975 to protest the appointment of UT's first woman president. Lorene Rogers was a biochemist who served as interim president of UT starting in 1974 and as president the next year. Not everyone welcomed her promotion, with some contending that they had been denied a voice, but she served in this difficult position until 1979. (PICA 10238.)

This six-foot card was gifted to the Longhorns in 1979. The service organization Silver Spurs manage Bevo, the longhorn mascot, and his transportation. Bevo is a well-loved and widely visible icon of UT, and this organization has been popular since its inception in 1937. (PICA 28508.)

The esteemed Longhorn Band is shown in action on October 7, 1971. The band started small in 1900 and grew quickly; by 1917, it was big enough to tour other states. Twenty years later, the band had over 200 members and has continued to grow. (PICA 09625.)

A group has gathered at the Tau Kappa Epsilon (TKE) Red Carnation Ball in 1982. The TKEs were founded at UT in 1951. Aside from social festivities, fraternities and sororities at UT are involved in various philanthropic and service activities. There are now as many as 70 national fraternities and sororities among the more than 1,000 student organizations on campus. (Lance Avery Morgan.)

Pictured in 1981 at a fraternity party are, from left to right, Deborah Wommack, TKE member Lance Avery Morgan, Allison Rice, and Tom Schwartz. Morgan recalls that Pres. Ronald Reagan had been a TKE, and there was a lot of buzz because of that. Also the *Animal House* film was still popular at the time, so interest in Greek membership was strong. The space program was robust in Houston, and Morgan had many fraternity brothers from Clear Lake and Houston whose fathers were NASA engineers and scientists. (Lance Avery Morgan.)

Here is the entrance to the Cactus Café inside the Texas Union Building, one of Austin's great acoustic and live music traditions. Since the café opened in 1979, it has acquired a national reputation. The walls outside the Cactus are adorned with posters from acts that performed there. (Author's collection.)

Scholz Garten, a beer garden, is shown here in 1971. This spot is always packed on game days. It was established in 1866, just after the Civil War. At first, it was a hub for German immigrants, but with a location between the university and the state capitol, it was quickly adopted by hungry and thirsty college students and politicians. (PICA 24462.)

On May 7, 1970, Les Amis Café opened at Twenty-Fourth and Nueces Street, just one block from the University of Texas. Past students remember it fondly, and Dennis Hopper, Art Garfunkel, and Jack Nicholson have been customers. A few scenes from the movie *Slacker* were filmed there. But a booming economy and steep rent increases caused Les Amis to close in 1997. (PICA 08569.)

The Varsity Theatre, pictured during its last days in the 1980s, opened in 1936. For the next 54 years, it was one of the theaters on Guadalupe Street across from campus. But over time, more students had cars and lived farther from campus, so attendance dwindled at the nearby theaters. The Varsity closed in 1990. Also shown are the stores Bazaar and Yarings, which for a time catered to the student population. (PICA 24697.)

This 1970s photograph is of the Renaissance Market across from the university. In the 1960s, artists and others sold art and handcrafted goods on the Drag. What had been informal became an established open-air bazaar in the 1970s, when the city set aside space. (PICA 01208.)

This Renaissance Market mural was painted by artists Kerry Awn, Tom Bauman, and Rick Turner in 1974. The murals on both sides of the market have been repaired since then and continue to add vibrant beauty and interest to the area. In this one, Stephen F. Austin stands at center holding an armadillo, surrounded by several Austin landmarks like the University of Texas Tower. (Author's collection.)

Perry Castañeda Library, opened in 1977, is the main library at the university and is one of the largest libraries in the United States. It is named after both Dr. Carlos Castañeda and Dr. Ervin Perry. Perry was the first African American to be appointed as professor at the University of Texas at Austin, as a civil engineer of distinction. Castañeda was a librarian and professor of history, and served as the first curator of the Latin American collection at the University of Texas. (Author's collection.)

Sid Richardson Hall, dedicated in 1971, is named after the successful Texas businessman and philanthropist. This lengthy building houses the Dolph Briscoe Center for American History, the Benson Latin American Collection, the Teresa Lozano Long Institute of Latin American Studies, and the Lyndon Baines Johnson School of Public Affairs. (Author's collection.)

Jesse H. Jones Hall, named after the Houston businessman and generous donor to UT scholarships and Memorial Stadium, is pictured with the adjoining Walter Cronkite Plaza. Cronkite enrolled at UT in 1933 to study political science, economics, and journalism. He wrote for the *Daily Texan* and served as an afternoon sports reporter at KNOW-AM, the campus radio station. (Author's collection.)

BIBLIOGRAPHY

Berry, Margaret Catherine. *UT Austin Traditions and Nostalgia*. Austin, TX: Eakin Press, 1983.

Botter, David. *University Goes to War*. Austin, TX: University of Texas Press, 1942.

Coe, Michael D. *Breaking the Maya Code*. New York, NY: Thames & Hudson Inc., 2012.

Eckhardt, Carl J. *Directory of Outdoor Statuary*. Austin, TX: University of Texas Press, 1988.

Frantz, Joe B. *The Forty-Acre Follies*. Austin, TX: Texas Monthly Press, 1983.

Morse, Frederic C. *The Ex-Students History of the University of Texas in Pictures*. Austin, TX: University of Texas Press, 1970.

Discover Thousands of Local History Books Featuring Millions of Vintage Images

Arcadia Publishing, the leading local history publisher in the United States, is committed to making history accessible and meaningful through publishing books that celebrate and preserve the heritage of America's people and places.

Find more books like this at
www.arcadiapublishing.com

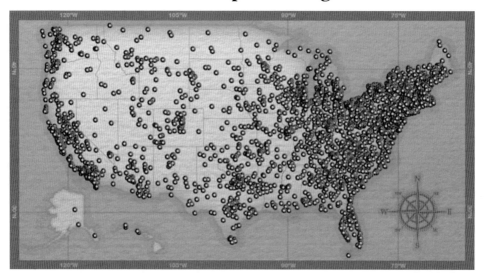

Search for your hometown history, your old stomping grounds, and even your favorite sports team.